# Endnotes

*by*

# Kelly Terwilliger

*Finishing Line Press*
Georgetown, Kentucky

# Endnotes

*for all my darlings*

Copyright © 2026 by Kelly Terwilliger
ISBN 979-8-89990-346-5 First Edition
All rights reserved under International and Pan-American Copyright Conventions. No part of this book may be reproduced in any manner whatsoever without written permission from the publisher, except in the case of brief quotations embodied in critical articles and reviews.

## ACKNOWLEDGMENTS

Many thanks

to *Willows Wept*, for publishing a version of "Another Bird."

to Arizona University Press for permission to use an excerpt by Joy Harjo.

Special thanks to Matthew Rowe who sent me the video of shoes in a tree, and to Zee H and Marlins Reigelberger who asked wonderful questions along the way. To Cori Kresge and members of her *Playing with Matches*—including Megan Williams, Sarah Skaggs, Wendy Osserman, Molly Gawler, Kev Abrams, and others—for inspiring inventiveness and creative risk-taking through the energy of their own work.

Warm thanks also to Karen McPherson, Eve Muller, Jeff Donaldson-Forbes and Carter McKenzie for their advice and encouragement on the final drafts of this manuscript. To my family, who embrace me and what I do.

And to Leo, especially, for endlessly cheering me on.

Thank you all.


Publisher: Leah Huete de Maines
Editor: Christen Kincaid
Cover Art: Kelly Terwilliger
Author Photo: Leo Cytrynbaum
Cover Design: Elizabeth Maines McCleavy


Order online: www.finishinglinepress.com
also available on amazon.com

Author inquiries and mail orders:
Finishing Line Press
PO Box 1626
Georgetown, Kentucky 40324
USA

# Contents

Poem ............................................................................................. 1

Illustrations ................................................................................. 3

Endnotes .................................................................................... 20

# Poem

Shoes in a tree, the bare tree
the shoes twirling a little.  A bird somewhere
singing in another conversation. The sky
seems so empty sometimes
even with clouds, the sky I love
sometimes frightens me.  I'd like a little welcome,
but here are shoes, swinging
above the fence too high to jump,
and the empty court, courting sun,
and shadows of clouds moving like exhalations,
and I'm thinking of people playing, maybe shouting,
everything moving
and the ball shoots wild and they

go with it, leaving their shoes behind.

I want this to be joyous, but something keeps shaking its head.
The space where they were is twirling
like a memory.
There is new invention in the time of longing.
But I can't see it yet. Maybe it's like huddle:
what didn't exist on a football field, or anywhere else
until the athletes who didn't hear sounds
gathered to say in signs
what they would do
when everything started moving again.
The field. The lines. The planets.

And then we all learned to make huddles
like this, rooms within
the rooms of us to focus courage in.

Shoe tree, when is this
in the course of your story?
Every now is always the beginning
and the middle and the end of something.
It is after whatever happened.
It is now unfolding its arms,
It is before they return and put on their shoes and walk across the sky.

Today I learn to sign *name* and *understand* and *no* and *why*.
In the woods yesterday I found the last place a bird sat
before it surrendered a spill of feathers.
Then, and now, and later,
we are pulled to gather around the fallen
in a kind of huddle. Where is spring now?
The buds are opening here.

And somewhere, little goats are coming down
from the hills into empty streets. Like questions,
curious, curious, unafraid.

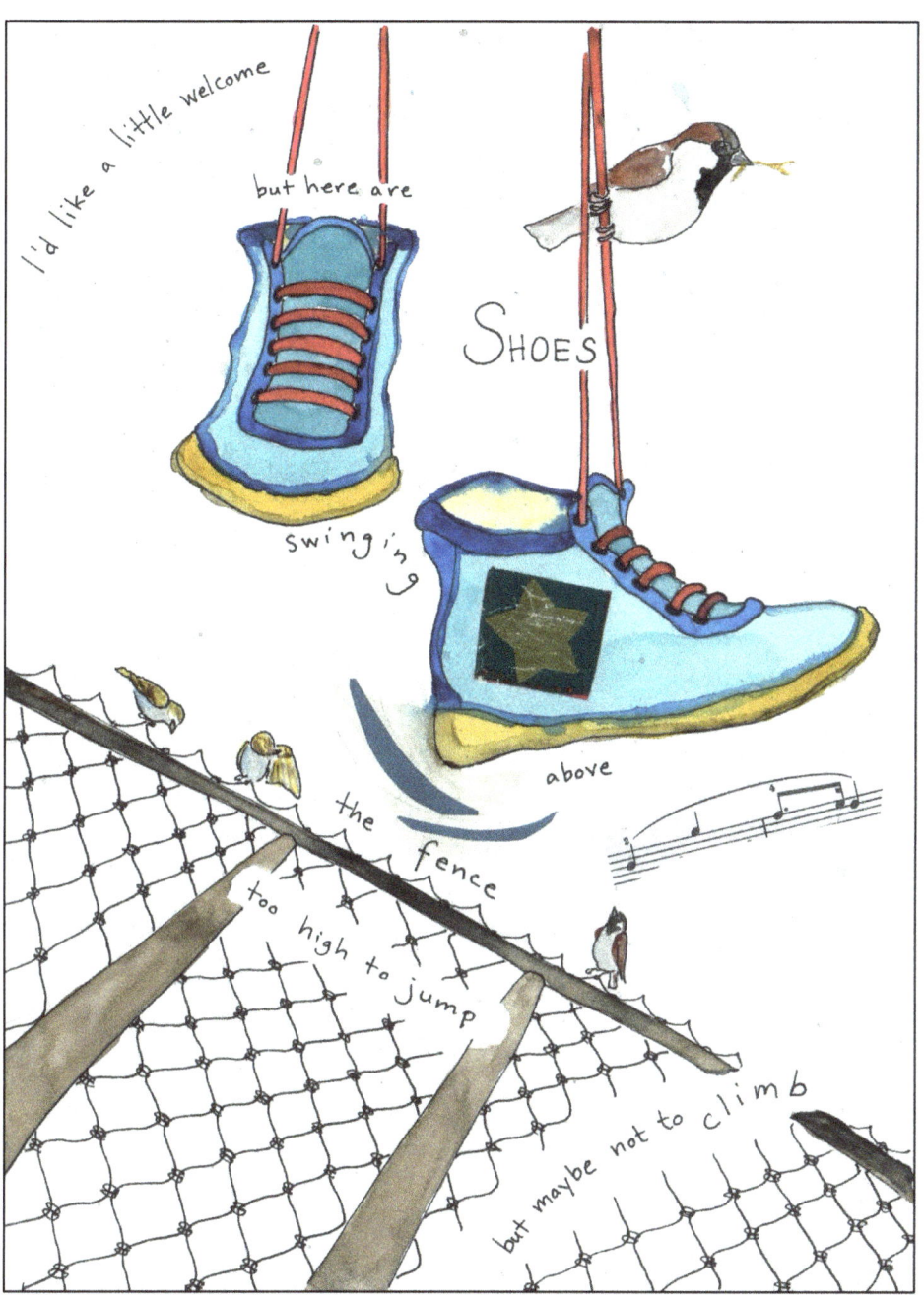

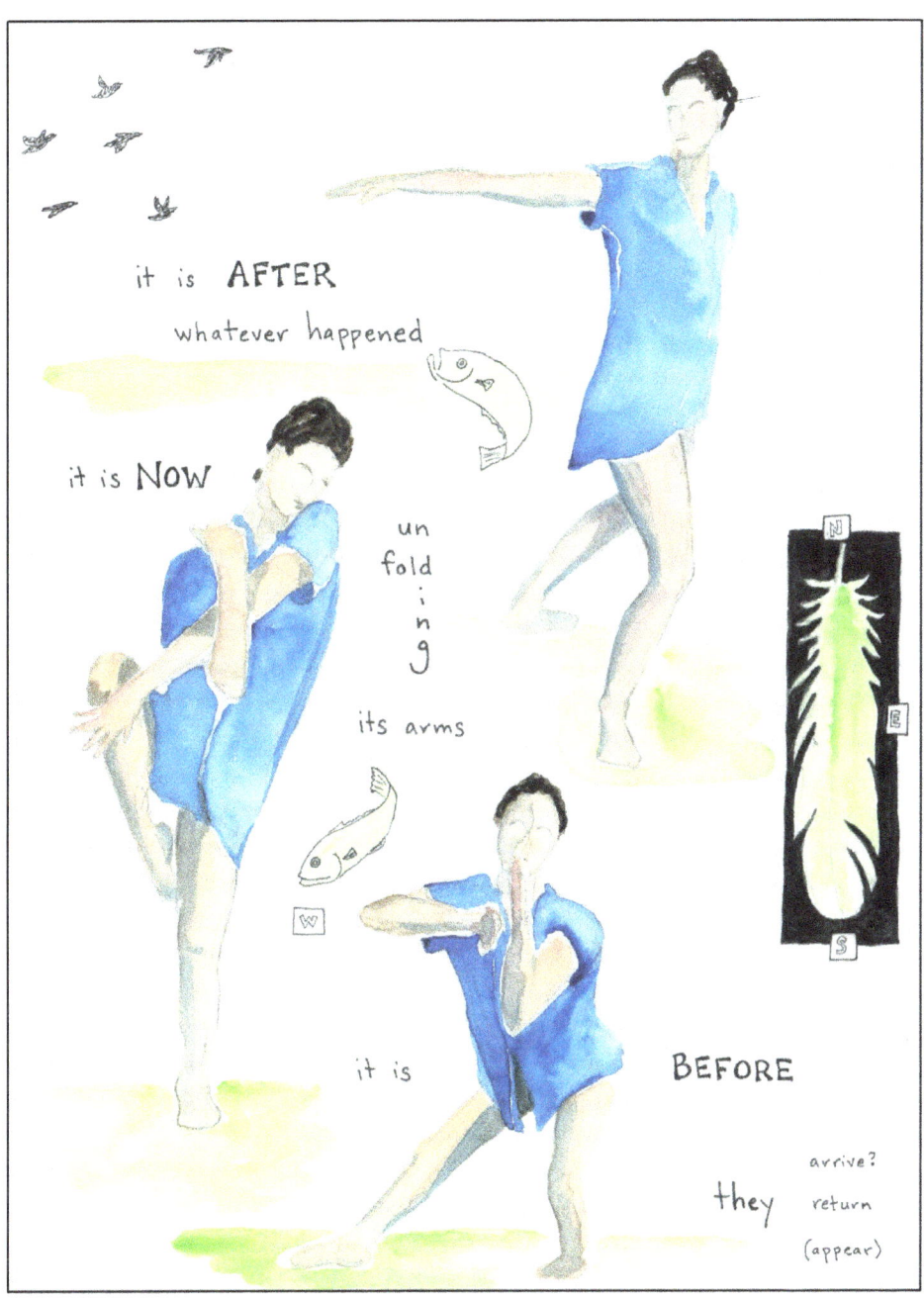

# Endnotes

ANOTHER CONVERSATION

The sound of droplets blowing down from branches rain-glazed, the sound of rain shaking out her hair, going wherever rain goes when she is done.

I am listening to a bird enumerate the hours until dark. One hit the window yesterday, hard, hard, how could there be anything left? I found her panting under a fern, eyes glazed. She was not the bird I expected. Smaller. Her grey head not grey but bluish, like certain clouds. Or, time of day: almost dusk, almost now.

Her green a complicated green, as if translated through several languages, one word relating to the thin skin of certain endangered trees, another to the taste of cinnamon, a third amounting to something like brevity, uncertainty, looking both ways before and after you cross a path. A fourth, being either the hopelessness of living forever or the possibility of change; a fifth, the look passed between people who don't know whether to trust each other but want to, and finally, the difference between a sun-lit and cloud-lit field of weeds.

I imagined her heartbeat in my hand. I watched her eye drift to the other side, then open again. I wanted to stroke the feathers.

SHOE TREE
Shoes in trees are signs. They don't mean what they mean on the ground. They carry some new significance, but if you don't know what it is, the shoes won't spell it out. They swing in the air, suspended. What once carried weight *is* weight, now. If shoes accumulate, they may become a conversation, or a story. Whatever they carry gathers emphasis by repetition. Shoe shoe shoe shoe. The wind blows. The shoes move, full, empty, back and forth.

RIDDLE
*Separate, we carry the same load.*
*Later we sleep, side by side*
*under the bed. What are we?*

> A riddle is an unnamed metaphor. Posed by one person it requires the response of another to be completed. Pleasure lies in "solving" the puzzle, the aha! when you see the connection another has laid out for your discovery.

> *Once, on a long car ride into the scrub and sage of high desert, my sons and I played a game: one person started a "riddle" without knowing the "answer:" "It has four eyes and a leg…" The others had to come up with a satisfying response. A riddle, inside-out, wholly collaborative. Discovering a "meaning" we didn't know when we started.*

> Go ahead—What has four eyes and a leg?

THE BEGINNING
I sent videos of rain, and bird sounds, and wind from Oregon to New York. I received rustling plastic bags, a rusted post-hole digger, a tree full of shoes.

It was the end of March, the beginning of April. The country had just closed down. Reports poured in: people falling sick, people dying. The populace sheltered at home. The streets emptied. We were waiting. For something to come roaring through. Maybe invisible. Maybe silent. But wouldn't we feel the air bend as it surrounded us? Wouldn't we feel time rush again sometime soon as the current pulled at the branches, the billboards, the empty cans left in the street? Didn't we hope we would hold on? That it would go by leaving us intact in its wake? Wasn't that a long time ago?

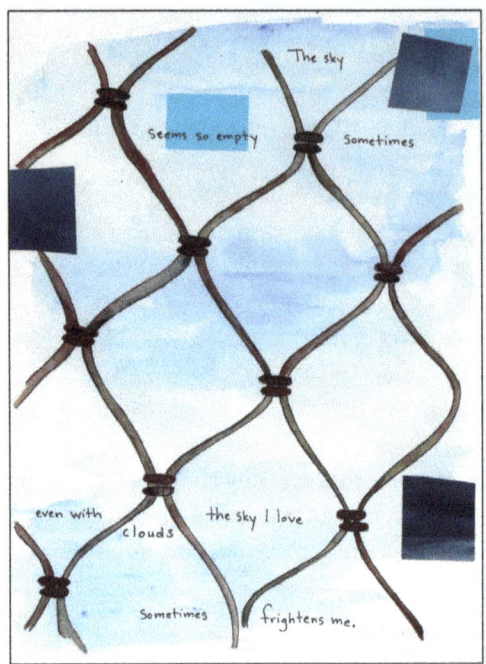

## THE SKY
There is a certain sky. For years I have tried to name it and cannot. It is a blank, the clouds high in the wind. Changing fast. It does not see me. Chain link fence. A flagpole, the clip on its rope hitting the metal. A dull clank. Repetitive, but not breath, not the ocean. It is the sound of not-there.

John Constable, British landscape painter, wrote to his friend, John Fisher, in October 1821: "I have done a great deal of skying…it will be difficult to name a class of landscape to which the sky is not the key-note, the standard of scale, and the chief organ of sentiment."

But sometimes a sky is no help. Sometimes its grand abstraction is too empty.

## CLOUDS
Leonardo da Vinci once described clouds as "bodies without surface." Of course: they have no skin. Their form, unstable, dissolves and coalesces, accumulates and vanishes. Like feelings. Like thoughts. They slip through the grasp of precision.

> (difficult to identify the moment of intersection with a cloud)

PRECISION AND EDGES
In visual art, an *edge* occurs where light changes. Maybe a surface bends or curves so that its sides are differently illuminated and the edges are thus visible. Or one surface stands in front of another, one brighter, one darker.

An edge can be *closed*, so that you see a clear visible change, a line, where the edge occurs. Or an edge can be open, which means you know there is an edge—there must be! There is a pear! There is a wall behind it which is not-pear! And yet one part of the pear blends in so completely with the wall that your eye passes seamlessly between them.

Sometimes it is hard to let myself see what I am actually seeing.

TEMPORARY
    Back when I was collecting clouds, I saw many skies
        I couldn't keep. Light
leaking
between minarets of condensation.

And then the wind, and the road
    turning, again.   Here, I said,
handing a camera back to my son,
        see if you can get that one
        out the window to the west—
the power lines
    streaking by, the truck
looming its wall of secret cargo, the sky
        tilting, caught by his temporary hands.

SEEING
When I was a child: that sky, that chain-link fence, the existential sky-feeling goes back to then. The fenced playground of my elementary school, and the enormous sea, down the hill, hidden by trees. The sometimes sad smell of those vast tides, metallic, like the taste of a lost tooth, the taste of tears. The day I wore my first pair of glasses to school, it was hard to keep them from falling off when I jumped or whirled or ran. I had something to guard, something holding me back, this fragile, loose, not-me, now-me. And worth guarding—each leaf had

become overnight its own separate perfection, each twig, each feather, each fingertip, the edges of things so finely formed, so visible. Nothing blurred into anything else. The world dazzled. I could see it all.

CLOUDS, AGAIN

The problem with photos in books is size. This should be enormous, but here's a tiny window, on a page, with sky.

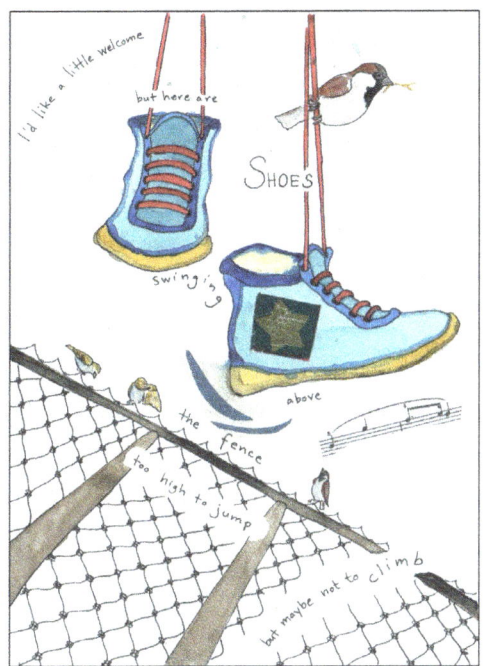

## HOUSE SPARROWS

House Sparrows, also known as English Sparrows, also known as European Sparrows. I put them in the painting because the tree is a city tree and house sparrows are city birds. After I'd painted them, I learned that the first house sparrows arrived in New York from England in 1852, eight pairs of them, brought (on a boat…the cages swinging) to control the out-of-control linden moth whose larvae were consuming city trees. Some sources say the sparrows did the job; others say nope, house sparrows don't eat linden moth larvae.[1] Either way the birds settled right in. They loved New York. They pretty much love anywhere people settle, having lived among us for at least 10,000 years. I see them in the parking lot of the grocery store I frequent, always busy. Always unfazed, it seems, by the large and moving world around them. A blink, a shrug, they dart away from cat car dogdog shoppingcart manlookingatphone broomhandle bootsole rockskitter truck truck garbagebag shoppingcart shoe shoe   shoe   to continue whatever they were doing.

## BIRDWATCHING

My friend's a serious birdwatcher. I am not. I just like seeing birds. Once you

---

[1] I later read that while adults may prefer grain and seeds (and crumbs) they often feed their chicks insects and larvae. (Rob Dunn, "The Story of the Most Common Bird in the World," *Smithsonian Magazine*, March 2, 2012)

start keeping lists and consulting e-bird charts and maps and travelling hours from home in hopes of a single bird sighting, it's not just that you like birds. You like something else, too. Maybe the challenge, the mastery, whatever compels people to "collect." You seek the rare, the rarely seen. A house sparrow is not usually worthy of attention. My birdwatcher friend and I nonetheless have a game: whatever bird happens to be in our field of vision at any moment is "my favorite bird." "My favorite bird" celebrates anything, everything.

BIRDWATCHER
*Why do you think you like to watch birds?*
*That's a good question... When they come into focus, they're... beautiful.*
*To see even a little bit of them, to recognize them, feels like a gift.*

Other lives. Alongside.

GOOD QUESTIONS
*How are you?* This should be a good question. *How* am I? As in, *how did I come to be here? How do I continue to exist? In what way, how, am I myself today?*

But, it's a gesture, part of a ritual. Who expects an answer? Often we don't want more than a ritual response. Like birds calling, across a distance: *I am here. I am here. I am here.* —So am I.

RECOGNITION
*The act of knowing again.*
Or, *re-cognition.* Knowing again, in a new way.

LIKE HUMAN BEINGS
Like human beings, house sparrows are social: they roost in groups, build nests in clumps, engage in social bathing and delight in social singing. That's when you all hop in the same bush or tree or thicket and just sing like crazy, all at once.

They dare to live where and as humans do: socially, successfully taking up space. This does not earn our admiration. We seem not to like species that resemble us. Search *house sparrows* and right away you'll find articles about pest control, warning that sparrows are nothing but trash birds. Carriers of mites and mess, killers of other better feathered friends. Stealers of other nests. Defacers of public property. Dislodgers of roof tiles that, falling from roof height, could easily kill a person. One site actually lists death by falling object as a danger posed by house sparrows. There are no recorded cases of death by sparrow tile. But we are invited to hate the possibility and to preemptively kill its perpetrator.

Other articles suggest relocating "problem" sparrows. You can make a substitute nest from a basket or plastic jug. You attach this close to the original nest, then scoop out nest and chicks and transfer them to the new location. The parents usually find their chicks within half an hour.

People have very strong and opposing feelings about the worth of sparrow lives.

ANOTHER BIRDWATCHER[2]
Christian Cooper, birdwatcher, Black man, was looking for Scarlet Tanagers[3] and Blackburnian Warblers, colorful birds moving among the branches: *glimpse, glimpse.* It's a game of intersections. What flickers in the foliage. What stands out. What the eye sees. Sometimes it's the whole bird; sometimes only a part, sometimes, not always, enough to identify the whole.

RECOGNITION
*Identification of someone or something from previous encounters or knowledge.*

Sometimes you can recognize a bird by the sound it makes. "When your mom calls you up on the phone, she doesn't have to say, 'this is your mother.' She just says, 'hi, dear!'…and you know instantly who it is. It is the same with the birds." (Christian Cooper, *Good Morning America*, YouTube, June 17, 2020).

Sometimes a gesture, a gait—you know it from a distance, even before you see a face.

RECOGNITION
                    (the face *lights up*)

(or not. SUSPICION:
        The White woman who intersected Christian Cooper's bird-watching

---

[2] Sarah Maslin, "How Two Lives Collided in Central Park, Rattling the Nation," *The New York Times,* June 14, 2020.

[3] There are no Scarlet Tanagers where I live, but their counterpart here is the Western Tanager, yellow and orangey-red instead of red-red. The Western, like the Scarlet, nests on the branches of trees, out from the trunk, where an elbow might be if tree limbs articulated like jointed arms. The nest is the flex-point: the location of a turn, something living on another trajectory.

thought he looked suspicious, meaning he looked worthy of another's suspicion. Hers. Meaning she thought he was suspect. A suspect. Which really meant she suspected. She was suspicious of him. Her suspicion made him suspicious to her. Suspicious of. Suspicious to. Slippery word. Slippery thought. How it joins us by separating us, suspiciously.)

SIGNS AND TRANSLATIONS
Ancient Egyptians had a sparrow hieroglyph.

Possibly it meant *small, narrow,* or *bad.*
Not generous.

But possibly it meant a *prolific man.*
Prolific in what way? Many offspring? Ideas? Beautifully carved objects? Harvested lemons? Money? Laughter? A "prolific man" can probably afford to be generous…but isn't, always. And *generous* comes from *genus* meaning *stock*, or *race*, so that *generous* was originally applied to one of "noble birth" and became part of a complicated dynamic of hierarchy. We could just use a different word: *Big-hearted. Open.*

Third translation: the sparrow hieroglyph meant *the revolution of a single year.* Sparrow as a measure of time, traveling through space.

WHAT WE DON'T KNOW
The sparrow in the picture is singing a scrap of melody from Robert Schumann's 1838 *Kinderszenen (Scenes from Childhood),* the first of which is titled *Von Fremden Landern und Menschen (Of Foreign Lands and Peoples).* The music is deceptively simple: easy to play the notes but hard to make them sing.

What are foreign lands and peoples to a child? *What is the world like where it is not home? And the people, what are they like, those I don't know?* Mostly imaginary.

> THE SMELL OF PARIS
> *When I was a child, a family friend went to Paris and brought back for me a box of sugar mice. Perhaps they were sweets meant to be eaten. I think now they were sweets meant to be eaten, but they were very beautiful, and so I never ate them. Small, perfect, sugar-crystalline mice I could hold in the palm of my hand. Did I touch one with my tongue? Maybe…the smell was sweet and foreign. It came from far away and*

*there was no name I knew to describe it. Would I know now? Would I recognize that smell today? Whenever I opened the box of sugar mice it was there; they had brought the faraway with them.*

*Now I look up sugar mice: a traditional sugar candy popular in the United Kingdom. Perhaps the "smell of Paris" was never Parisian at all. That little box was its own country, for me forever mysterious.*

"Foreign lands and peoples" are always imaginary to some degree. Or they would not be foreign. But what if time goes by and one forgets that the imaginary is still imaginary?

UNRESOLVED NOTE.
And when for some the whole world feels like *not-home*, and people everywhere like *not-my-people*, then what? Where does such a person turn?

SHADOWS

A body in relation to the sun. In relation to time, the rotation of a day, the revolution of a year. How a body is positioned within the light of the world. A shadow trails behind, looms in front. A shadow, barely noticed underneath.
    (There are other sources of illumination that occur in the mind.
    There are felt shadows that require no light at all.)

FORESHADOW
To give an indication, a hint of something to come.
    (Note: The shadow cast in front of a body is never exact.)

BASKETBALL
The ball against paved ground
the thump and faint
sing of it, and feet—fast STOP. Fast-fast-fast STOP.
Stopping and starting, the ball, the feet. Hands. Hands. The clap
of contact: pass-clap, pass-clap, pass-clap. And then
ball and ground, drumming, drumming, singing again. It hits
the board, another drum whose pitch shifts
depending on where you strike it: bam, bonk, bank, thonk. It dings
the hoop and twangs, it slips the net like air, like water,
it comes out gleaming, but you, we,
can only hear it—here: the air
is singing. Alive again, a snake has shed
its skin, the game makes itself again.
Bounce-bounce. Slap. Thonk. Swish.[4]

---

[4] Where are the sounds of the people breathing? one of my friends asked. The aliveness, she said, behind all the other sounds. I realized yes: the people are missing. I painted them, but really the poem is haunted by their absence. I suppose I am haunted by their absence. Sound was my effort to conjure them, but *they* did not materialize.

## MORE CLOUDS

A week into pandemic quarantine, it happened. One day my eyes were full of clouds.

Now, they come and go. The surface has not changed, but often it seems like there is something. Between my looking and the world beyond my eyes. There is an interruption. Through which I must consider what I am not-seeing. *I want to brush away it / won't be brushed away my/ vision/ I brush/ has always been partial*

SHADOWS

(These are REFLECTIONS inside shadows. Which makes them twice wonderful.[5])

---

5 REFLECTION: What a surface throws back, light or heat. Or an image produced by the action of light bending, curving, folding back from a shiny surface. Reflection inside a shadow: light blocked and bounced at the same time.
    (Reflection: pondering some subject, again)

## SKY SWIMMING

The swallows come in the morning from wherever their lives are. They fly as if through water, to the higher windows, and land and cling to the wood that divides windows into window lights, window panes. They look like visitants, their white bellies pressed against the glass, their tiny masks, their greens and purples glittering in the darkness of their wings. They look, it seems, right at me, speaking in high voices, opening and closing their odd short beaks made for plucking things out of air. A fine rain sifts down. The swallows let go as if releasing from the tiled edge of a pool to dart off swimming again, fast, through a morning full of not quite empty spaces.

## VIOLET-GREEN SWALLOW

They had never done this before, land repeatedly on the window frames. I wonder if one landed first by mistake, thinking that the window was more sky and the frame a perch with air on all sides? How strange it must have seemed. To press one's belly against solid air. Perhaps then others learned to do the same. They spent a lot of time chittering over their shoulders at each other. *Look at this! Here the sky is shiny and you can lean against it! –Ooh! Move over, Let me try!* Or maybe they were giving directions, or passing on news, or just singing.

They didn't notice me as long as I didn't move. I could stand very close on the other side of the glass and look at them without causing alarm, there on the other side of their sky.

SKY FISH

"Invisible fish swim this ghost-ocean now described by waves of sand, by water-worn rock. Soon the fish will learn to walk. Then humans will come ashore and paint dreams on the drying stone. Then later, much later, the ocean floor will be punctuated by chevy trucks, carrying the dreamer's descendants, who are on their way to the store." [6]
—Joy Harjo

> Joy Harjo, I love that these descendants are on their way to the store. To get some bread maybe, or some chips. *We're out of milk,* said the mom of one, we need some milk. Mundane, that's what this is. Mundane, *ordinary*: hot day, empty road, nothing moves out there except the wind, windows down, smell of baking vinyl seats rising up heavy-sweet. Same old store, same old stuff, same tired guy at the cash. Mundane, not exalted, just: *of this earthly world.* Joy Harjo, you give me plenty of time, plenty of time to let this earthly world fill with dust and fish and dreams and time, all its layers shimmering, the visible, the invisible.

SPARROWS AGAIN

The ancient Egyptians saw sparrows as intermediaries between the world of the living and the world of the dead, carrying souls of the deceased to their afterlife.

I've heard that Egyptian sailors tattooed sparrows on themselves in the hopes that their souls would be sparrow-caught even if they died at sea, far away from songbirds. Did they think the image would draw living sparrows to them? Or would the image itself carry them?

---

6 Joy Harjo, *Secret from the Center of the World,* UA Press, 1989, p. 46.

TATTOO
*The birds are etching their silver-pointed songs onto the skin of the day. By nightfall there will be no untouched surface left.*

*(What is an untouched surface?)*

SURFACE: This word is huge. Because there is so much of it. Because surface always carries with it the implication of what lies underneath it.[7] Not just a shadow, but another layer, another reality, possibly an enormous one. Even a bottomless sea has a surface…But not everything does. What about those clouds?

MORE SURFACES: Someone on the radio, I can't remember who or when, was talking about a British airship, back before the Hindenburg. The whole interior, the actual realm of passengers, was, he said, an illusion of solidity: everything had to be as light as possible…paper ceilings, fabric walls, pillars made of balsa wood. A floating world you could practically put your finger through. And the bags used to hold the hydrogen that lifted the dirigible? They were made of ox intestines. Nothing else worked so well.[8]

TATTOO (2): Today I remembered a character in a novel by Susanna Clarke.[9] My recollection was that the character had eaten a book, but it turns out I was wrong: his father had eaten the book on a dare, and it was a book of magic, so when the father fathered the child, the child was born with inscriptions all over his body. They became more pronounced as he grew older. They looked like tattoos, but they came from the inside, the inherited ink rising to the surface. He was a living book, but he could not read himself, and most often he chose not to let others read him, either. A book who actively evaded readers.

---

7 As a child I had repeating dreams in which the ground would suddenly be full of holes, gaps, fissures. Underneath was emptiness. There was no solidity I could depend on. Just a capricious surface.

8 Some googling led me to identify this airship as R101. A million and a half ox intestines. Imagine the musky odor they imparted to the ship and its veneer of opulence. The ship's brief flight, before it crashed and burned in France. Only 6 of the 54 people aboard survived. A second ship, R100, flew to Canada and back. But after the demise of R101, R100 was dismantled, flattened by a steam roller, and sold for 600 pounds as scrap, surface reduced to skin of a much smaller solid.

9 Susannah Clarke, *Jonathan Strange & Mr. Norrell,* Bloomsbury Publishing, 2004.

POEMS WITHIN POEMS

I saw the window, the light, the sleeper, the fish—and then realized they had appeared in another poem, already written. I am sorry I didn't paint the nets from the already-written; they could have echoed all the chain-link fences. I got lost in the curtain, the dark room, the daylight outside. Imagining the curtain breathing. Inside, outside. The light half-entering. Perhaps the curtain is another kind of net through which some things pass, some do not…Isn't this a good game? Everything can become another kind of something else.

> Two discuss the price of fish, or maybe
> just exchange a little news. Or advice needed so much
> there isn't time to put the fish down,
> scales shedding into palms, sour and salt,
> the eyes gone flat, already slipped to that other world
> the souls of fish drift through, I don't know what
> to do, one says, she won't get out of bed.
> And the other with the big hoop earring says, baby,
> give her time. And the wind moves the bright red folds
> of clothes and dries the stiffened gills of fish and brings
> the sound of voices and something clanking, ringing.
> The sea unfolds itself, a girl somewhere turns on her pillow,

the wind touches the glint of fish scales on the arms of friends who
bend and glitter, their voices low, the world shaking
down around them those nets
through which we go and go.

*VOYEURISTIC*
A friend, when she read this poem, thought it seemed somehow "more voyeuristic" than other endnotes. Maybe because the viewer of this scene is not in it, not situated in relation to the people confiding, someone sleeping, the sense of trouble tangled all around—the reader is only part of this scene through watching it unfold. This relationship occurs when reading most third-person writing and watching much staged or filmed performance. We watch. We stare at whatever we're given.

In 'real life" we are taught not to stare at people we don't know. And yet, we need to be aware of others, to see each other, to consider lives that aren't our own. And we need to step back and look at ourselves, from time to time, from a distance.

Where is the line between *voyeurism* and *witnessing*? When does the other stay *other*? When does the other become *you*?

THE SPACE WHERE THEY WERE
The jar of dried citrus a friend dropped by
gleams on the counter of disarray
slices of orange, lemon, tangerine packed
behind glass like fanciful wheels, fortunes, the imprints
of beasts from a previous epoch. I miss
the little goats and their mischief
that stayed here once in those years before
the neighbor moved away and killed himself. I miss my innocence.

I miss the bookshop owner, my friend because I buy his books
and ask about his morning and remember his birthday
he's an autumn baby and here it is, wet, wet spring, and the shop is closed
because they all are, we're *distant* now, plus he just had his kidney out
so he's home, hoping to find his balance.
I imagine that new space, that confusion of organs
inside takes some getting used to, and I want to send him chocolates
but I don't know where he lives besides among those books, I miss
the books. I miss the smell of them. I miss my friend who spent one term

learning to play the pipe organ. The hard part, she said,
was the time it took the air to travel into sound.
The pipes waiting, silent, then booming out, a while after.
You had to keep doing whatever you were doing
even though what you heard around you
was already in the past. You had to keep moving into that other time
the one you felt beneath your fingers, beneath your pumping feet,
to keep what came after from breaking.

> (Someone was talking on the radio about the ruins of Notre Dame Cathedral and how to rebuild not just a shape but a vessel of sound. The cathedral's organ survived the fire that destroyed the building, but its sound depends upon the space around it. As it happens, a map exists, a sound map. One night, after a concert, an acoustician mapped the specific reverberations and echoes of the entire cathedral space. I don't remember why. Why not? He did it, that acoustician, so now the space can be rebuilt to match that map of sound.)

> (*Even if they do, it won't be the same.* There were years of dust. And candle soot. The exhalations of all those thousands of visitors. All that, too, was part of the sound. Of course it won't be the same. It was never the same. It was always changing.)[10]

INVENTION
During the pandemic, there were scenes on city streets: refrigerators stuffed with free food, musicians playing free music in stairwells; people delivering gifts with fishing poles, wearing hats with pool noodles at outdoor cafes to maintain *safe spaces* while making each other laugh. Kindness, and the necessary playfulness of invention in adversity.[11]

None of these objects is new: refrigerator, stairwell, fishing pole, pool noodle, but re-purposing is invention. You are inventing a new use.

And what if an old use is brought back from disuse? This seems like re-invention. Not re-purposing, if the use doesn't change—but maybe re-enlivening.

---

10  See note to NOTRE DAME AGAIN for more on this. It's coming up in a few pages.

11  "[Play] makes us flexible. By reinterpreting reality and begetting novelty, we keep from becoming rigid. Play enables us to rearrange our capacities and our very identity so that they can be used in unforeseen ways." (Stephen Nachmanovitch, *Free Play: Improvisation in Life and Art,* Penguin/Tarcher, 1990, p.43).

RE-ENLIVENING
Kathleen Jamie describes a contemporary village, Quinhagak, in Alaska. The village sits alongside an archeological site, an ancient village that until recently was buried for half a millennium. The rising sea has been scouring the ancient village free of earth, revealing objects from another time. Pre-European contact time. The Yup'ik people participating in the excavation of this village are making replicas of forgotten tools and ceremonial objects. They are re-learning old approaches. They are finding their ancestral culture returning to them in recovered things.[12]

    (RECOVERED: uncovered/regained OR covered again.)

    (GAME:
    Choose a thing. A pencil. A rock. A cardboard tube…Anything.
    Make a list of ten different ways to use it.
    Now ten more.
    Now imagine that thing in ten different places.
    Where does it look most dignified?)

THING THEORY
It sounds so good, "thing theory." I wish I had invented the name. There are things and there are objects. Things simply exist. *Objects* are things we use and define & understand through our use of them.

The culture in which I live mostly confronts the thingness of objects when they stop working the way we want them to.[13] And, because we are interested in things for the ways in which they are useful to us or illuminate our understanding of ourselves, we mostly don't really see things as anything but objects.

REGARDING THINGS
Other cultures see all things of the world, animate and inanimate as possessing "soul."

It seems to me the more you divide the world into things and beings worthy of respect and those simply worth their usefulness, the more likely you are to take, to claim, to use, to possess without consideration or gratitude.

I JUST CAN'T SEE IT YET

---

12  Kathleen Jamie, *Surfacing*, Sort of Books, 2019.

13  …and therefore when we are probably most grumpy and annoyed with them.

We were standing in the yard in front of the house, just a little dry grass, and across the street, a high wooden fence. Behind the fence, two girls were jumping on a trampoline. Their gleeful voices, a wing of hair flapping up, down, a wave of an arm, a bit of clothing, billowing, descending. The toddler beside me was busy picking weeds. A couple of birds flew by, above us, in silhouette.
Look, I said, pointing. Birds!
The toddler looked up. Are they alive? he asked.
Yes, I said. Of course they are.
How can I know? he said. I can't see their eyes.

How was that child seeing the world? I can't ask him now; that thought is so long ago slipped away, that thought from the time before we remember thinking.
How do I define *alive*?

SEEING AND THINGS
I'd been looking for a book and couldn't find it anywhere. One of those things that escapes notice even when you are trying to see it…and then, there it was, leaning against another. I opened it up, and, Mark Doty, if you ever read this, just know I have loved your little book for years. I read, "by looking very hard at an object it suddenly comes that much closer to some realm where it isn't a thing at all but something just on the edge of dissolving." And later, "what we are is attention…a bright point of consciousness in a wide field from which we are not really separate." [14]

---

[14] Mark Doty, *Still Life With Oysters and Lemons*, Beacon Press, 2001, pp 6 and 68.

HISTORY
The American football huddle (and many other huddles) in which people gather close and face inward for collective focus, plan, or energy, was reportedly invented by Paul Hubbard, a quarterback at Gallaudet University in 1894. Gallaudet was among the first schools for deaf and hard-of-hearing students. Hubbard realized that his hand signals could be read by opposing players, particularly those from other schools for the deaf. The huddle was his solution. And it spread. Hubbard's huddle became mainstream, ubiquitous.

TWICE
On this page the "figures" progress vertically in two columns, while the words do their usual left to right horizontal thing. When this was pointed out to me I considered re-doing the image. I really do like things to make sense! I really do like a sense of order.

But I decided not to change the picture. It requires "reading" twice, in different directions.

HUMMINGBIRD NEST
The Calliope hummingbird makes a nest on a branch or even a conifer cone. Moss, shredded bark, plant down, covered with lichen, bound with cocoons

and spider silk, lined with plant fluff. A recipe from another world. Old nests are often renewed, used again. Hummingbird, you weigh two, maybe three grams, a fraction of an ounce. You fly thousands of miles. You find that one branch, that scrap of nest again. If it hasn't fallen. If the tree is still standing.

There are many almost invisible parts of this world that are known. By someone. A hummingbird, say.

## CALLIOPE

Hummingbirds are generally named for the sound their wings make. The Calliope (cal-eye-ope-ee) is specifically named for the muse of eloquence, of epic poetry. *Calliope* means "beautifully voiced," and the epic she inspired was poetry spoken, sung, told. Beautifully, with her help. Why did John Gould, English ornithologist, name a tiny bird, notable for its relative silence, *Calliope*, muse of beautifully-voiced epic poetry? "Mysterious," *The Birder's Handbook* notes, admitting bafflement. For this, I love *The Birder's Handbook*.[15]

## CALLIOPE (2)

If you pronounce it *cally-ope,* it denotes a steam-powered musical instrument played with a keyboard. It shoots air through locomotive whistles of various sizes. They are very loud. Uncontrollably loud. Not fireworks and explosions loud, but the sound of fairs and circuses and riverboats. A noise that carries to draw people from a distance. To bring people together in hopes of a lively time.

## CALLIOPE (3)

She was not just a muse. She was Chief of the Muses. She was also the mother of beautifully-voiced Orpheus. He sang and everyone stopped to listen. He sang and the dogs went quiet. He sang and the birds grew still in the trees to hear him better. He sang and the trees bent toward him, the stones awoke and soaked his singing in.

## THE UNDERWORLD OF DOUBT

> When Orpheus went to the underworld to bring Eurydice back to the living, he almost succeeded, his singing was so beautiful...Go, said Hades. She will follow. But don't look back until you've passed through the gates to the world of living.
> Orpheus went, but the path was long, and the silence grew behind him.

---

[15] Paul Erhlich, David Dohkin, and Darryl Wheye, *The Birder's Handbook: A Field Guide to the Natural History of North American Birds,* Touchstone, 1988.

Are you there? he called. No one answered.

At the gate he paused. As soon as he stepped through, the underworld would close behind him. If Eurydice wasn't there, he'd never see her again. He would lose his only chance, and what if she was not there now

and what if the god had deceived him

and what if he could make sure make sure make sure

he turned—

and there she was.  And wasn't.

She saw him    her smile it

was as if                    did she say

      goodbye or did he       just imagining

voice again, her

shadow  she was only

a shadow    if only    he had       without looking back—

## DOUBT

It paralyzes. It undoes. It reminds me to consider other options.

Here, doubt erodes resolve, and there, it opens fruitful wondering.

In one moment, the unknown horrifies; elsewhere, uncertainty offers the space of mystery, possibility, curiosity, exploration.

## ANOTHER SPARROW

The Venerable Bede, in his *Ecclesiatical History of the English People,* written around 731, tells of a sparrow flying through a mead-hall where fires blaze and people sit at supper: the bird flies in one door, he says, and out another, and that tiny warm passage through the hall is like a single human lifetime. The winter storms raging outside the hall are the time *which is unknown to us.*

I'm thinking about the sparrow, where it came from, where it was going. I'm thinking how, when you huddle close to a fire, everything else gets so much darker. The surrounding world almost seems to close, *click*, like a screen, like a wall. You are in your huddle. But if you step outside your eyes adjust. Often, the rain does not seem as heavy when you let yourself be part of it. You can smell the wind. You can be out there.

    Can you? I have left Bede's metaphor. I have left his mead-hall, his before-life, his after-life. Am I walking into the unknown, or avoiding it?

## ANOTHER RESPONSE TO DOUBT

(Listen to: "Do," read by Andrew Scott. A letter from Sol LeWitt to Eva Hesse, letterslive.com)

## THE FIELD

This painting went through more transformations than any other. It has a different feel. Transformation, the chaos of transformation, the chaos of motion, commotion—the tumble of life tangling with life. The flat football field becomes a hillside, flying, birds, petals, rivers of space. Oceans. And over this, the globe, the city, a single person, balanced for a moment, words interrupting words. The colors kept changing in this painting, *no*, I thought, and I'd try again, the books—are they blowing away or coming toward us? The glimpse of stars.

A huddle is only temporary. We have to go on. Step out and everything starts: the sound of the steam organ, *calli-ope*, wheezing and hooting down the river, the wind blowing voices clamoring stories stories stories bumping careening combining growing softer louder muffled whirling changing the wind plowing the water blowing the banners shouting scraping singing ricocheting the words cannot hold together the sense cannot the form gives way to motion wild a roar of—

Of course, this is only one imagining. You could also step out Focused. Aware. Ready to perform the perfect _____. Grounded. Solid.

At peace, even. Serene.

Or.

WORDS
Looking again I am inclined to change the scraps of words on this painting to new ones, the ones troubling me now. Or to leave blank spaces so that every time this page opens words can be added or exchanged. Words of anxiety, nonsense, necessity. The little word joineries that hold the others together. Words of color, texture, fragrance. Musicality. Pieces of platitudes, pieces of lies, pieces of fury and kindness.

> KINDNESS: A word I've pondered before. How it relates to
> KIN (clan, tribe, family; the Indo-European root "to give birth to"),
> KINSHIP ("blood connection," or feeling of connection to anyone),
> KINDRED (as in like, related, close, not necessarily by ancestry. *Kindred spirit*),
> KIND (defined by resemblance, similarity. And: good-natured, warm-hearted, caring, considerate).

> (following paths of words as if they were a map unfurling into other times, other layers. It's a backward map: what words used to mean, what holds them up from underneath, how they connect to other words. A map of retrieval. Re-cognition. Rubbing away the surface in order to find the echoes overlooked or forgotten. The connections we lean upon without always noticing that we lean.)

These endnotes are a map slowly revealing itself, a kind of thought-scape in the process of coming into being. "Maps," say Katherine Hammon, "…bear implicit promises of routes into and out of the unknown."[16] Where am I going? Will I come back? A map says yes.[16]

But isn't a map that reveals itself as you go simply a path in the making? You can't know where it is going. Where is the big picture? This is the glory of a map: You are here. In relation to…But an unfolding path offers only the path and whatever you can see from it.

> (PREPOSITIONS: words that map, that let us locate things in relation to things)

---

16 Katherine Hammon, *The Map as Art*, Princeton Architectural Press, 2009, p. 9.

## KALEIDOSCOPE
This word comes to mind when the world feels like it's whirling. Many pieces, colors, voices, bodies of people, bodies of things, emotional, rotational, sensational collide-o-scope.

And yet, a kaleidoscope is all about order. Its carefully tilted internal mirrors create a perfectly symmetrical visual array out of broken scraps. You put the tube to your eye and turn it and everything falls to pieces, the little pieces slide into new positions. Then you see them: all the same pieces, rearranged. A new array. New proximities made beautiful with repetition, reflection. *Kaleidoscope* means "beautiful seeing."

A *teleidoscope* (cross between telescope and kaleidoscope) does not have little colored pieces built into it, but instead reflects the outside world into symmetrical designs. Chair leg, leaf shadow, stop sign, dog on a leash: pieces appear again, again, again, meeting like the folds of a snowflake, becoming strange and beautiful in their reflected turnings and joinings.

I like the idea of these rearranging mirrors, and I enjoy the experience of seeing the colorful complexity they create. But I don't stay interested very long: when I look through a kaleidoscope (or teleidoscope) I'm only temporarily enchanted. Color and design move from chaos to resolution, but the same kind of order is repeated every time. Turning and rearranging changes the positions of pieces, but not the structure of the whole.

## NOTRE DAME AGAIN: SOUND MIRRORS
So, I looked it up: the acoustician in question is Brian Katz, and his map made clear that the cathedral was really a kind of mirrored funhouse for reflected sound. Sound bounced off of everything. And was…beautiful. Some people think that the acoustics of this sound mirror palace inspired polyphonic music—music in which different voices sing different notes at the same time. At the time the cathedral was built, monks sang single melodic lines in unison. But the reflected sounds inside the cathedral were such that these single lines overlapped and mingled and resonated and harmonized. New patterns emerged.[17]

---

17 See "How to restore the legendary acoustics of Notre Dame," by Emily Conover in Science News, January 12, 2020. The whole article is amazing.

PAPER BAG
This could be a mistake, this painting. Its sudden return to stillness.

But why not? The wild simultaneity of the world includes stillness. Why not a paper bag nest, nested in a cluster of trees, just now?

Don't we all have unspoken places (outside, inside) to which we return to be ourselves? Where we might go to reconsider. To change direction. To reflect. To remember a direction we'd forgotten.

    (places where we cease to *perform*)

(Maybe those places, wherever they are, are home.)

ALDERS
Red alder, *alnus rubra*, of the birch family. They grow along the Pacific flank of northern North America, tracing the edge of what we call The United States and Canada. They grow in my dreams, late in the day, a thrush is singing from somewhere among them. The bark of young trees is smooth and blue-grey, with blotches of white. But red alders are named for what is underneath this skin: the reddish inner bark which shows when a tree is scraped or bruised,

cut open. This red makes a dye which renders nets invisible to fish. A tea of it is medicinal. The wood, having no strong flavor of its own, serves well as bowls and spoons for holding human food. The burning wood does not scatter sparks. The smoke is the smoke of choice for smoking salmon.

Alders grow fast where the earth has been disturbed: fire, mudslide, clear cut. The bottomland next to the house where I grew up: empty, and then, alders, growing faster than we did. Slender companions we climbed, my brother and I, and near the top, we swung. (Like Frost and his birches, though we didn't know either, then.) Just the green world rustling, swaying, the earthy, sour scent of bark rubbed in, children and trees we were flapping, flapping, held by underground roots to the face of the earth.

They grow fast, alders, but they don't live long in the lifespans of trees. Their roots prepare the earth for others: fixing nitrogen, producing anti-fungal toxins. Other tree species depend on them. And alders themselves live in clusters. Social trees, in the company of each other. Their roots touching. Passing along alder information.

PAVEMENT

*The primary function of a pavement is to transmit loads to the sub-base and underlying soil. Modern flexible pavements contain sand and gravel or crushed stone compacted with a binder of bituminous material, such as asphalt, tar, or asphaltic oil. Such a pavement has enough plasticity to absorb shock.*
—Encyclopedia Britannica, https://www.britannica.com/technology/pavement-civil-engineering


BITUMIN, TAR, ASPHALT

They are all dark brown or black, viscous, sticky liquids. Bitumin, a tarlike substance, also called asphalt, comes from coal. (Although asphalt can also refer to bitumen mixed with sand or gravel, ready for road making.) Tar? It comes from coal, wood, petroleum, peat. "Destructive distillation," is how you achieve the transformation, using high temperatures to break down large molecules into new structures. Tar is sometimes called pitch. Pitch, when produced by plants is also known as resin, and some kinds of resin are known as rosin. Rosin is used by players of stringed instruments. Rubbed on bow hair it allows the bow to grip the strings and make them speak, or vibrate clearly… And so we go from ancient trees which are the source of coal, to coal, to tar, to roads, to trees, to the sound of another instrument, speaking.

ROOTS AND PAVEMENT
The picture I've painted isn't realistic. Let's be clear on that. Do I really think that roots can go right down through concrete pavement as if it were cake? According to GreenBlue Urban, the formula for the space you need between an urban tree and the "hardscape surface" is 3.5 x DBH (Diameter in inches of mature tree at Breast Height—although whose breast height is not specified). This helps avoid root heave, which happens when soil compacted for the purposes of bearing city weight leaves roots with nowhere to go except to squeeze just underneath the lid of street. Soil has an "architecture," made of the arrangement of particles of various sizes, and the gaps and voids between them. These gaps are where life enters. With "suspended pavement," you support pavement with struts and sections which allows you to keep the spacious architecture of soil underneath for that realm of roots we don't see and easily forget until they break our surface.

Lid, surface, scar. How much can live under paved ground? How much do we suffocate in creating our own ease of motion in the world? Our wide streets were once alive. And yet, even the path I take through the woods exists because footsteps have packed it down. It is a visible path because nothing grows there. I'm not sure what to do with this. I'm not sure, sometimes, what to do with my own feet on the ground.

READING
I love this kid, and the book. Could be me, someone I know. You. Or someone I'll never meet. Reading. This is another intersection; being in two places at once. Your body sits on a bench, holding your place in this world, while you think someplace else.

MEANWHILE THE SPARROW

"…depends on humans to such an extent it might be reasonable to say it is native to humanity rather than to some particular region." (According to Rob Dunn, "The Story of the Most Common Bird in the World," Smithsonian Magazine, March 2, 2012.)

SPURV   (Norwegian, Danish)
ZWEZO (Haitian Creole)
GEALBAHN (Irish)
CHAMSAE (Korean)
URABEC (Bosnian)
SPATZ (German)
UNDLUNKULU (Zulu)
SUZUME (Japanese)
KELE (Hopi)
GORRIÓN (Spanish)
NZA (Igbo)
PIHOIHOI (Maori)
CHUNCHUQ (Uzbek)
SHIMBIRTU (Somali)
HARABEL (Albanian)
BURUNG GEREJA (Indonesian)
KANATAKÓN:HA (Mowhawk)
CHIM SÓ (Vietnamese)
MOINEAU DE MAISON (French)

## STORY MAP

This is a map of an instant in the midst of a story. The map, the moment, points in many directions. How it looks and where you go next depends on where you stand now, and also how you begin to describe what you perceive.

Here, a body dances the map. We could use sticks as well. Or paint. Or tin cans. We could use an array of sounds: car door, crickets, laughter, wind chimes, faucet running, stopping. We could bend grasses. There is string. And also wedding cake, wax beans, ashes. A brief map made of rotting fruit. Wet footprints. The lines on hands, the lines radiating from the corner of an eye, (crow's feet), a map in motion: a leap, a map traced on the surface of a lake. A map made of blackberry juice rubbed onto a forearm, a map of hair, woven, of feathers stuck into wet sand, aluminum tubing, broken glass reclaimed, chewable vitamins, a map in the tangle of Queen Anne's lace that grows by a roadside I know in August.

A map of a story can show many things. How people or events are located, relative to or related to one another: a map of place. How events unfold: a map of time. Both of these together. A map of kinship, friendship, enmity; a map of moods; a map of thoughts; a map of rash choices, a map of every time someone forgets their shoes, or laughs aloud, a map of quirks. A map of grievances, sorrows. We could go on like this, forever.

MAPPING AND NAMING
When I was a child, my friend and I walked around her neighborhood and made maps. Okay, let me clarify: we were extra-terrestrials, come for a visit. We arrived in space ships that looked like large cardboard boxes. We emerged and explored with the imaginary eyes of far away. We left no traces. We took possession of nothing, we renamed everything we saw.

A STORY, A SONG, A POEM IS THE EXPERIENCE OF A MAP
*When you are telling a story I can see it in my mind. I feel like I am there.*
    This is when you know you've told it well.

A STORY, A SONG, A POEM *IS* A MAP: The Aboriginal People of Australia are famous for their songlines, song spirals, stories that move through a lived landscape.

"[The stories] do not move in one direction through time and space. They are a map we follow through Country as they connect to other clans. Everything is connected…"

"Song spirals describe everything, so that you see it, you know where it is, you could go there and gather it. Song spirals are a route. Song spirals walk through the land."

—from *Song Spirals: Sharing Women's Wisdom of Country through Songlines,* by Gay-wu Group of Women of the Yolngu People, Australia.[18]

DANCING THE MAP
The body is simultaneous. In this place. And indicating that remembered place, or the one anticipated.

TIME
The me of this book will never change, once I stop writing it. (Now the fawns are running down the path I can see from the window, first one, then the other. The other stops to scratch an ear, then hurries to catch up. They disappear from my view and I am wishing I could go with them, or that they would return and dance a little nearby the way they did in early spring. Already their white spots are fading, the grasses have gone to seed…) The you of this book will

---

18 Published by Allen and Unwin, 2019.

be different every time you read it, assuming you return more than once. And because of you, this meeting place of a book will be different, too…The book is a point in the map of the encounter. Wherever, whoever you are is the rest of that map.

CITY AND FOREST
The city is a forest of towers. The forest is a city of trees. I come from forest country, can you tell? Every city in my mind, at least in this poem, has a forest somewhere beyond it…not true, of course, for the world at large. Maybe your cities have deserts beyond them, or mountains, or fields, or more cities. Or just stars…

WALKING ACROSS THE SKY
I don't know. Are they spirits? Walking across the sky?… Or just kids, on their way somewhere?

> (A poem:"Summer Somewhere," in Don't Call Us Dead, by Danez Smith, 2017)

Let them be whole. They have climbed the fence. They have found their shoes. They are unconfined. Un-threatened. Maybe they will land in the city, over there, or the forest just beyond. Maybe they will keep walking to another place we can't see…Everyone who has been waiting for them will be waiting there. A picnic. A party. A surprise for someone who thought they had been forgotten. Everyone will chant their names as they approach.

Maybe this can be the next story.

## THE OTHER VERSION

There was another version of this painting, but it didn't launch up enough. The fence filled up with details tucked among the spaces which made me want to stay and look at it instead of the sky. And a whole little neighborhood stood in front of the city. A garden, a swing, a beach, and a bench and an overturned boat. Even a tiny guy fishing on a little dock. I wanted to be there! I took it out because it was too inviting, and I knew those kids were going farther. I didn't want them to miss too much. And I didn't want to get too comfortable where I was and not let my mind go with them. Maybe that little neighborhood in the other painting is where they are going, farther on. Maybe we'll join them. But we're not there yet.

LEARNING TO SIGN
*See: Bill Vicars, ASL You Tube videos*

I watch the videos. I watch the man explain that some questions, yes/no questions, you ask with your eyebrows up. Others—where, how, when, who—you bring the eyebrows down. This makes sense. I move my eyebrows up and down and think about how questions feel. How it feels to wonder in this way, in that way, and how it feels to ask.

Asking a question is potentially two things: requesting to know, and admitting you don't.

Often these two things happen together.

But think of the questions that ask what is already known.
Think of the questions that admit not knowing without asking to know.

What are the questions I am forgetting?

NOT
It looked like a nest. No.
The feathers looked like flowers. And then I looked again. They were not.
Many feathers scattered means a bird has been caught, probably by a hawk.
In the forest, it's the small hawks who maneuver the spaces between trees:
here, *sharp-shinned* hawks; their Eurasian counterparts, *sparrowhawks*.

(A hawk flies through a space and all birdsong ceases.)

It was not a place of beginning, but a place of ending.[19] Not a nest.
Or, it was a nest: A place of sustenance for one, and a place of dying for another.

And the white feathers clung to the dirt and nothing else was left
of the bird that was or the bird that is.

>NOT/OR/AND
>Degrees of possibility: <u>*This NOT that*</u> is absolute. It does not allow
>for possibility. <u>*This OR that*</u> means you temporarily consider both. It
>might be a case of uncertainty—you need more information to know
>which one; or indecisiveness—you need to chose which one. In the

---

19 …or, becoming something new. Becoming hawk.

end, only one is possible, but OR lets them both hover for a time.
Finally, *this AND that* renders both possible, possibly at the same time.

ANOTHER BIRD

Bird, she-bird, downy
woodpecker hits the glaze
of window full\on and drops—oh she doesn't
suffer long: I watch her disappear.  I watch her
cease behind the surface of her eye.
It stops, like that. There's a wall
and there's nothing like a wall. My job now
is to see. Keep watching. If it changes
something. If it changes
nothing. The fledgling
jays fly to the same roof, not knowing, just feeling
the heat on their feather\fluff belly\down   belly down
they spread their wings and grin
like little kids. Look at me! Look at me, mom!  Death beside them
is just another feathered thing.
And I can't save   can't\save            can't\save
black and white her feathers       one wing
outspread like a hand     reaching
out and one small feather
tuft by her eye,   dancing
with the wind.  She doesn't blink.
They say the day will be a warm one
the tilt of the earth, its milky surface
blazing, blazing  I can't save

BRANCHES

The branches I saw were not actually branches. They were the roots of a fallen Douglass fir, enormous underground fingers now crooked around nothing. Even the earth that lifted with them when the tree tipped wasn't solid. It crumbled away into air under my scrambling feet as I climbed up to take a closer look.

> *WINDTHROW*
> A word for the complete uprooting of a tree by strong winds. This becomes more likely when the ground is very wet and soft. When a tree is already unbalanced. When they fall you can hear the cracking

from a distance. The ground shakes when they hit. The forest shakes. When one falls, the more likely it is that others will fall. They brace themselves together, and their roots are often intertwined.

ROOTS, AGAIN
It is thought that many trees exchange nutrients and even chemical information via roots that meet underground. Through these connections trees can support each other. The bark on the stump of a felled tree will sometimes grow up and over the "wound" to seal it, heal it. It is thought that the continuing circulation of nutrients from connected trees is what enables this.

STUMP
Sharp-shinned Hawks carry their prey to a stump or low branch to pluck it before eating. Swallowing feathers is not normal for them, as it is for owls. (Google: All About Birds, The Cornell Lab)

So, I was probably right about those feathers.

SHARP-SHINNED HAWK
They fly like acrobats. They anchor shallow nests between trunks and horizontal branches high in trees. These temporary dwellings are full of twigs, bark flakes, and chicks covered in fluffy white down.

EATING SPARROW
The Eurasian version is not called sparrowhawk for nothing. These and the sharp-shinned eat songbirds, and not much else. The males remove and consume the heads of their prey before presenting the rest to mate or chicks.

People do it too. Eat sparrows. Sparrow was a common dish in Britain through World War I, especially among those who did not have access to other sources of meat (thanks to a landowning class that severely punished poachers). Simon Wood, in *Birds of Essex*, describes the nocturnal pursuit of collecting roosting house sparrows in batfouling nets.[20] You found them sleeping in the ivy that grew on walls, or in the thatch of rooftops. If you stretched a net across an open door of a barn and banged the walls you could startle many at once. Enough for a

---

20 Alternate spelling: bat-*fowling* nets. Never intended for bats. These long-handled nets were used for catching birds at night after awakening them from their roosts.

whole pie.[21]

You cooked the pies slowly until the bones were soft enough to eat.

SPARROW PIE

Sparrow pie could also be a fancy dish. Perhaps this depended more on who was eating it and who was judging the eating than on the dish itself. In Britain, to be told that you had "dined on sparrow pie" once meant that you had made an inspired or intelligent remark; you became what you ate—you were sparrow-like. Lively. Quick-witted. Presumably this also only applied to certain classes of people.

---

21 For further details consult the Marsea Museum website's article, "Sparrow Pie at the Peldon Rose."

BLUR
What if this picture were all street? Or what if it were all woodland? Instead of merging the two together? How would those other versions feel?

Some people talk about urban development encroaching upon wild space. Some people talk about non-human species encroaching upon cultivated spaces.

> (More words to consider: development, cultivation, encroachment)

BLUE
Blue distance. Sky. Sea. Twilight.

An in-between some hills fade into. Shadows make indistinct.

A mood. A melancholy. A burden. A bruise.

*Black and blue.* Collision. Injury. Conflict.

I meant the blue figures to be offering comfort and support. I look again: how else could I read them? How might another do so?

BLOOMING
In the long spring of isolation, I saw things I hadn't noticed before. Leaves emerging, blossoms unwrapping, each day changing shape, opening, fading, falling away. Life in quarantine narrowed its radius and time altered. It didn't slow down so much as enlarge, blur. It became measured by small alterations I saw in things around me.

Another day shaking down more wet petals. They are everywhere, and then they are gone. Beauty beauty beauty. It keeps coming. Not the carved thing, but the light on it, the dust that moves, and settles, and moves. It is the apprehension—stand right here. Maybe it will come again—

TREE
I've switched trees. Or…combined trees. One is that shoe tree in New York City. The other is a wild cherry in my Oregon driveway.

SHOES.
These are my shoes this time. If you see them, let them mean what you want them to. The chicks sheltering in them, they can stand for whatever you need left shoes to carry.

THE SOUND OF NESTLINGS
For many years, I heard this sound and it didn't register. A high persistent sound, the excitement of seeing parents approach with food. *Feed me! Sustain me! Let me live.*

OTHER SENSES
I didn't spend a lot of time during this writing touching the plants I saw. They were probably happy enough about this. But there was a period of time when the forest was full of fragrances that had no obvious source. There was one spot in particular, and the fragrance (from nothing I could see) was so delicious I wished I could just stand there and feed myself by breathing deeply this delectable air…This lasted maybe ten days, and then it was gone.

I say a *period of time*. Actually, the forest has never been without fragrance. It just doesn't stay floral forever. The smell of new leaves, young leaves, the smell of fully opened leaves, the smell of aging leaves. Plants coming into fullness, plants fading—there are layers upon layers of time in the fragrances of living things I hadn't really considered before.

PLANE TREES

The tree in this painting is a London Plane tree, a cross between a Sycamore and an Asian Plane tree, thought to have come about centuries ago when a Sycamore and an Asian Plane tree were planted side by side. London Planes don't grow where I live, but I know them from cities elsewhere. They are tolerant of both air pollution and root compaction, so do better than many trees in urban settings. They are even rumored to remove pollutants from the air—thank you, Plane trees! Their flaking outermost skin likely allows them to expel such toxins more easily.

Their peeling patchwork bark! Whether it sheds the grime of the world, or simply renews a surface, it is a skin of scraps and ghosts of maps growing between tree and world. Or growing into the world. Through the world. There is a tree in a park in East London that has engulfed a small iron fence. A sign in the park reads "One of the oldest trees in the park is a London plane and it has a fence growing through it." The sign stands some distance from the tree—you are meant to go in search of the marvel the sign describes. But it is unmistakable: the old tree beside an old moat, and a fence. The fence disappears into the tree, and comes out the other side.

How interesting, to say the fence was growing…or even to say it "comes out the other side." As if the fence were the living, moving part.

PLANE
    1. a flat surface on which a straight line joining any two points would wholly lie.
    2. an imaginary flat surface through or joining material bodies
    3. a flat surface of a material object
    4. a level of existence or thought

from *planum*, meaning *flat surface*

A flat word full of joining.

    A DIFFERENT WORD, ACTUALLY.
    The plane tree actually gets its name from the Latin platanus, meaning broad.

COMPOSITION
I taped all the pictures in this collection to the north wall, in the hallway. There was space, and I could see them all together. One, two, three—had the same composition. What was this? Again, again, again? This was not intended. As I started shaping the last picture, it happened once more. I tried to reverse it, but it didn't feel right. I gave in. I am stuck, it seems, repeating this shape, this direction. Even the colors in these paintings echo each other. Perhaps they are trying to tell me the same thing and I keep failing to comprehend.

An opening, left to right. As if a river—coming through, flowing, a current, something spreading outward…In my language left to right is how words move, and the words on these pages, maybe they insist that the paintings move with them. A visual narrative: in my "language" time moves this way, too. One enters from the left and journeys to the right. If you enter from the right you are returning, making a reappearance. If I lived in another language, I could feel time and space differently, I am sure of it.

There is the landscape and there is the mind. We live in both and they create each other.

I am caught again by how I've learned to see.

DEER CROSSING THE YARD
Somewhere I wrote a poem about watching deer in my yard, walking, it seemed,

into the past, because they were walking from right to left. I don't think this holds true for my own body; only for what I observe. If I turn to the left or turn to the right I don't have the sensation of moving toward past or future. But watching those deer—I remember imagining them retracing steps, and perhaps entering time again, differently this go around.

ANOTHER MAP
The Wintu people of California use cardinal directions to describe their bodies rather than referencing left and right. "In Wintu, it's the world that's stable, yourself that's contingent, that's nothing apart from its surroundings." [22]

How would it feel to have my body so constantly located? Always in context? Something to try. My west hand reaching across the bed where I sit. My east wrist feeling a little sore. Already I like it. When I change position I think I will like the experience even more.

GOATS
What happens when we are gone? What happens to the spaces we leave empty? What fills them? This question we ask or don't ask as we temporarily leave places we have frequented. This question we ask or don't ask as the planet changes around us. This question we ask or don't ask when we look in the mirror.

NOT QUITE GOATS
*The gentle people in the Patagonian legend chose not to fight. I can give you weapons, their prince told them, and you can drive the others away, but in the process you will become like them. So instead they crossed the river, transformed, now four legs, now delicate nostrils raised to the wind. They left and did not leave.*

I can't decide how I feel about this story. It is a story of resistance through waiting—because, the story says, the gentle people will return when the greedy people are gone. How the greedy people go, it doesn't say. How long this will take, it doesn't say. I think I come from an impatient culture. I wonder if there is enough time. I wonder what will be left, even if there is. I want the gentle people now…and the story stands on the other side of the river, watching me, twitching its ears. Nibbling grasses for as long as it takes. The fist of our world clenches, unclenches. The heart passes its pools from room to room, auricle, ventricle, auricle, ventricle, the window now is open, the thunder comes at

---

22 Rebecca Solnit, *A Field Guide to Getting Lost,* Penguin Books, 2006, p. 17.

dawn, and the birdsong, too.

"REAL" WORLD
These painted goats came traipsing into a town in Wales in the midst of the 2020 pandemic when all the people had shut themselves inside. Maybe this will be a story that lasts, and maybe it will wash away with time. Who knows. When I saw the photographs and videos it was as if I were being offered a glimpse of another possibility, a future in which other lives with other forms would take our places, the world would not stay empty. Or, when the pandemic passed, we might re-enter the world differently. That this time of disruption, time of loss, might also be, for those who live, for life itself, an opportunity to do better, whatever that might mean.

"Return," like turn, always has the possibility of something new in it, even when it means coming back to something old.

> (Alberto Giacometti worked on a single portrait for eighteen days, every day undoing and redoing until finally he agreed to stop. Then he stood back. He looked at the painting. "Well," he said, "we've gone far. We could have gone further still…it's only the beginning of what it could be. But that's something, anyway.")
>
> (From *A Giacometti Portrait* by James Lord)

OUT OF REACH
Something happens as you make a thing. It changes as you make it. Maybe there is a vision, but the closer you approach the vision, the more it drifts to the side, or just ahead of you. The perfect thing stays out of reach. Perhaps there is no perfect thing. Perhaps it was always an illusion. Or perhaps there are thoughts that change as they take form. A kind of translation occurs, and you end up with the thought, expressed, only it is not quite as you had expected. It is a little tilted. Or a lot. Maybe when Emily Dickinson said to tell the truth but tell it slant, maybe there isn't really a choice. Coming into being will slant whether you will it to or not.

CURIOUS
What does it mean to be curious? It comes from a word meaning *careful*. Eager to know, to learn. It is akin to wonder and wondering. The sort of surprise that doesn't take fright and run away, but thinks about what it's seeing.

What would we need for our questions to the world around us, to each other, to ourselves to become *curious*? What would we have to put aside? What would we gain?

And, what then?

**Kelly Terwilliger** grew up on the Oregon coast. Her family of marine biologists taught her to pay attention to shifting places of life: tidepools, mudflats, beaches—and to appreciate the traces of intersecting lives therein. A bottom drawer in her family's small kitchen became her art drawer, full of scrap paper, scissors, crayons, and glue. She made quill pens out of feathers she found on the beach and the mineral scent of India ink became the smell of written words.

Kelly is the author of three previous collections of poetry, *A Glimpse of Oranges; Riddle, Fish Hook, Thorn, Key,* and *Night Maps.* Her work has appeared in journals and anthologies in the US, Canada, and Britain, including *The Atlanta Review, december magazine, Raleigh Review, Amsterdam Review,* and *Sarabande.* She won first place in the Guernsey International Poetry Competition in 2025, and she was awarded a residency at PLAYA in Central Oregon to work on a collaborative writing project about swimming in wild places. Kelly also teaches and performs as an oral storyteller.

With *Endnotes*, the translation from words to images to notes becomes what Kelly sees as a map of mind. The book offers a path, while also suggesting the unspoken spaces around that journey—the terra incognita made of quiet and chaos, others' untold stories, and pieces of self and universe yet to be noticed.

www.ingramcontent.com/pod-product-compliance
Lightning Source LLC
Chambersburg PA
CBHW040253170426
43191CB00019B/2401